Royal

Biographies
Volume 7

Prince William and Prince Harry

2 Books in 1

Katy Holborn

Table of Contents

Prince William

A Prince William Biography

Katy Holborn

Prince William

A Spotlight on the 'Reluctant' Royal

Even before Prince William was born, the eyes of the world were already trained firmly in his direction.

His mother, Diana, was a shy, stunning beauty who had captured the heart of the heir to the British throne. The fresh-faced aristocrat worked as a kindergarten assistant and was only 19 years old when they fell in love – or, in Prince Charles' infamous words after their engagement was announced, *"Whatever 'in love' means."* Her romance with Charles would propel her into an entirely different life from the quieter one she knew as Lady Diana Spencer. The shy English rose was suddenly cast in a role few people in the world are really equipped for – that of leading lady in a fairy tale everyone desperately wanted to end in happily ever after.

There was a picture-perfect wedding in July 1981 and shortly after, in November of the same year, a joyful announcement that a child was on the way. She was only 20 years old at the time, already navigating the minefield of modern royalty meshed with modern celebrity, treading the line between the public and the private.

As mother to a child slated for the throne of a powerful country, it was of no surprise that everyone was paying close attention to the pregnant princess. But Diana stoked interest on her own merits too. With her beauty and quiet charisma, coupled with a warmth and openness unprecedented in the royal family, the public simply couldn't get enough of her. This fixation would only intensify with her pregnancy. Later biographies and interviews of the princess would reveal her feelings about the pressures of carrying a royal child – as if the world was watching her stomach. As if she was being monitored daily. As if the whole country was with her in labor…

In many ways, she was right. Fixations with the royal baby bump and the pressures of carrying a child in line to the throne were not new of course, but hers was a different time. The 1980s presented economic uncertainty, cultural shifts and heady changes for the British people. There was far less deference to the monarchy. There was greater freedom of speech. The iconic punk band, the Sex Pistols, for example, had released their provocative single, *God Save the Queen* just a few years prior in 1977. With lyrics like *"She's not a human being"* and *"There's no future,"* it was brash, disillusioned, anti-establishment – and a veritable hit that would be remembered even now, not only as one of the greatest songs of all time and for its seminal part in shaping Rock and Roll, but also for capturing a sense of the era. Part of that times was characterized by a monarchy that seemed crippled by rigid formality, out of touch, and somewhat detached from the tougher realities faced by most of the country.

But then came Charles and Diana's fairy tale, and in Diana, the arrival onto the scene of a modern princess who was forging her way beneath the limelight – and into people's hearts. When she became pregnant, she had also taken on a symbolic relevance, as a writer for the *New York Times* would eventually put it; her pregnancy was a link to the past and a promise for the future. A pregnant princess, it seemed, was a literal embodiment of a sense of continuity for the monarchy.

Even before Prince William was born, therefore, he was already carrying the hopes of his people on his shoulders. He already had burdens and faced high expectations.

The 1980s was also an age of technology, information, celebrity, and consumerism. There was insatiable public demand for information on and photographs of the royal family and consequently, intense competition from press outlets. This, in turn, would foster relentless media attention that would only deepen for the Royals over time. That attention would never leave them, and in particular, would hound Diana, the People's Princess, even unto death.

Princess Diana suffered under that media scrutiny brutally. Later, Prince William would reveal in a candid documentary, *Diana: Our Mother*, how crying over press intrusion was a regular occurrence for the Princess, who had been chased, blocked and even spat on by the press that constantly hounded her. Intense though it may have been for Princess Diana, however, she was in the public eye mainly after being romantically linked to Prince Charles. She had, in a sense, 19 years of relative freedom before that. Their son Prince William, on the other hand, would be subject to the glare of cameras all his life.

He was a baby in his mom's belly when photos of Princess Diana in Barbados, wearing a bikini while pregnant, made worldwide headlines when they came out in 1982. The press would be there on Prince William's first day of life too, camping outside the hospital where he was born, well placed to catch a photo of him when he was presented to the world as a baby covered in a plush white blanket in his mother's arms. There would be photos of him growing up, dressed for school, trying to live a normal life while caught between feuding parents. There would be unforgettable, heartbreaking images of him walking behind his mother's casket in her funeral procession. She was famously killed in a car crash partially attributed to a gaggle of paparazzi photographers who had all but chased her to death. There would be revealing photographs of his wife, Katherine the Duchess of Cambridge, while sunbathing in private on vacation. Racy photos of his brother, Prince Harry, enjoying a wild night out with friends in Las Vegas would also come out. There would be cunning means of acquiring photos of Prince William's children too, including actions that could be considered stalking and allegedly, the use of other children to bait the youngest royals into a playful photo op.

Royals of any age have always led interesting lives, and people have always been interested in knowing all about them. Our history books, for instance, are bursting with anecdotes of the eccentricities and misbehavior, of the trials, triumphs, and tragedies, of many royal figures long before this generation. But the public's current access to information, as well as its sense of entitlement to receiving them, is unprecedented.

Prince William's mother, Diana, stepped into the limelight upon her romance with Prince Charles. The royals before them were able to have more private lives, due to limited technology and more public deference to the monarchy. Now, there are telephoto lenses enhancing the reach of cameras. Data can be hacked and leaked, phones can be tapped and conversations recorded. Everyone has a smartphone with camera and video. Everyone has become a potential paparazzi.

Based on his family history, it shouldn't come as a surprise to anyone if Prince William had a bit of a bone to pick with the press (as he is accused of having). But as modern royals with limited actual power in government, the family also has an understanding of their symbolic roles; and part of symbolism is imagery and public access to their lives. They know they have to work with the media. In this way, the family has learned, and is continuing to learn, how to live with and leverage the power of the press to be able to do their work and pursue their advocacies.

Undoubtedly, many more authorized and unauthorized photos and information are still in the cards for the royal family in the future. But they're making compromises too, like agreeing to more public events in exchange for more respect for their private moments. They've also made surprising and very modern strides forward, for example in announcing the Duke and Duchess of Cambridge's third pregnancy via the social media platform, Twitter and having official social media accounts. Though the royals' social media presence is externally managed very proper and sometimes impersonal, it is still a sign of this family's constant ability to adjust and move with the times to stay relevant. The Royal Family has an account, as does Prince Charles and second wife the Duchess of Cornwall via Clarence House. And for inquiring minds - yes, they all use hashtags!

By the time Prince William takes the crown as King, we will have a man on the throne with unparalleled amounts of documentation on his life, available on all forms of media. There will be photos and videos, press releases, magazine articles, books, documentaries, movies and TV shows, and 140-character statements, even. He will certainly be amongst the most watched royals of all time.

We don't have to wonder about the accuracy of royal portraits painted by master artists, we have photos of Prince William aplenty, in every age. We don't have to dig up and decipher old letters and wonder about salacious love affairs; "William + Ex-girlfriends" are but a few clicks away on a search engine. We have so much information that we can even find the former relationships of his wife, and the former relationships of their former relationships. When it comes to Prince William, we simply won't have to dig so deep or scratch our heads in too much mystery. If anything, we have more information than we know what to do with.

True to the information age Prince William lives in and will one day reign in, the problem in understanding the life of a royal so deeply entrenched in the public sphere, isn't so much that we have limited information, but what, from all the data that is out there, can be counted as relevant information?

In one of Prince William's most famous photographs growing up, we see him in an apron and we know he was cooking chicken paella at Eton. Of the famed 90s girl pop group, The Spice Girls, we know he may have had a poster of "Baby Spice" Emma Bunton on his walls. He is apparently bad at video games, calling himself *"enthusiastic but quite useless*" as a gamer. And speaking of gaming… he was interested in acquiring a Playstation, but needed to figure out how his wife felt about it first.

These are just random trivia that show we know so much and see so much of the young royal who will one day be King. But what can we really make of what we've seen? We think we have an idea of him as a son, as a husband, as a father. But what is important of all the information that is out there? What are the key events that have shaped his life, and how might he be as a monarch? Is he really, as some in the press have alleged, a "reluctant royal" who would rather have a quiet life in the country? Could he be "work-shy" with light hours and limited loads, especially compared to his grandparents, Queen Elizabeth and Prince Philip, who have stayed in grueling public service well into their 90s? Is he really restrictive of press freedom? How will he be working alongside the government, while maintaining political neutrality as royals are expected to be?

Of all the quantity of information that we have on Prince William, what is really worth knowing about the man who is second in line to the throne?

Charles and Diana's Son

On the 21st of June, 1982, a boy, the eldest child of Princess Diana and Prince Charles of Wales, was born. Prince William Arthur Philip Louis, is second-in-line to a throne over 1,000 years old. He has a rich life ahead of him, but on the morning that he was first presented to the public, on the steps of London's St. Mary's Hospital very shortly after his birth, the 7-pound, 1 and ½ ounce boy was just a little blue-eyed baby in a blanket, in the arms of his parents.

His father, the reserved Prince Charles, was 33-years old and his mother, the shy Diana, was 20. They were young and beautiful and looked delighted. They married just a little over a year earlier in July, in a lavish ceremony viewed by millions of people all over the world. It was just like a fairytale, and the birth of their child, a son and an heir to the throne, was just one more piece in the picture-perfect puzzle of the happily ever after everyone was craving. Over the years, i would become painfully clear to all that behind the scenes, that was not at all the case. By some accounts, even the early years of their marriage and the duration of Diana': pregnancy were far from idyllic.

Even before Prince William was born, he would already be experiencing the tumult o: his parents' stormy relationship. In a candid conversation revealed later by the National Geographic in a documentary titled *Diana: I: Her Own Words*, a despondent Princess shared how she had once been so unhappy that she threw herself down a flight of stairs while pregnant. It was a cry for help and it would not be her last one along the course of her troubled existence behind the gilded walls of her palace life.

In this way and in many others, there would be no discussion of the kind of man William is, without first looking at the life of his parents.

A "Crowded" Marriage

Lady Diana Spencer, as daughter of Earl Spencer, had a privileged life. It was plagued by the marital woes of her own family, but she was a beautiful woman with a pedigree, and moved in the rarified circles of the royal family. Her older sister Sarah had even caught the eye of Charles, the Prince of

Wales, and they dated for a time. While that relationship ultimately came to nothing, Diana too would catch the reserved royal's attention. He was in his early thirties and she was 19 when they began a relationship in 1980.

The young woman fell under heavy media scrutiny, and by some accounts, Prince Charles' father, the royal consort Prince Philip, would write to his son and encourage him to either settle down with Diana or to let her go, out of consideration for her reputation. Prince Charles, who may have interpreted the missive as a command, proposed to Diana and the couple would marry shortly after her 20th birthday in July 1981. Later reports would reveal they both entertained reservations before taking that dive into marriage – after all, they did reportedly go on just 12 dates before getting engaged - but the ceremony itself was stunning and captured the imagination of the world.

Unfortunately, it was all a collective fantasy that would unravel equally publicly.

Diana gave birth to William a year after their wedding, in 1982. William's younger brother, Prince Henry Charles Albert David, would follow two years later in September 1984. Even then, however, it seemed the relationship between their parents was crumbling. Charles was reportedly not enthusiastic about the redheaded baby boy, and Diana believed her husband had already resumed a relationship with his long-time love (and now current wife, the Duchess of Cornwall), Camilla. Things would only deteriorate from there, in spite of everyone's desire to see the marriage work, including efforts from Prince Charles' parents, Queen Elizabeth II and Prince Philip, at an intervention.

By mid-1992, biographer Andrew Morton's seminal *Diana: Her True Story - in Her Own Words*, was released, and it was apparent to many that the Princess had actively participated in its writing. It is searing and authoritative. The dirty laundry was out, and it wouldn't be the last to be aired publicly. Later the same year, the so-called "Squidgygate tapes" were unleashed to the world… a conversation between the Princess, nicknamed "Squidgy" by her friend and alleged lover, James Gilbey, and the man himself, who would say it several times throughout the record. This was followed by an official visit to South Korea, where the dynamics of the relationship was watched closely – from their glum expressions to hostile body language - and deemed doomed. The official announcement of their separation would follow shortly after their return home.

Morton's book became a huge bestseller, and its subject, Princess Diana, appeared to the public as a sympathetic, tortured figure. A vilified Prince Charles did not help himself when a work-related TV documentary for the Prince's Trust that aired in 1994, eventually turned into a more personal interview, with a revelation on adultery when his relationship with Diana deteriorated. Though damaging, this is a far less shocking affair than the "Camillagate" tapes leaked earlier, in which recorded phone conversations would reveal the Prince reportedly joked about wishing to be his lover's tampon.

But Diana was not done with her own revelations. In November 1995, she fired back with a tell-all interview before journalist Martin Bashir of the BBC. The Panorama Interview, as it would eventually be known, was unflinching, brutal and unforgettable. She admitted to infidelity, shared her struggles with mental issues, and had said the now-iconic, "*There were three of us in this marriage, so it was a bit crowded.*" Some royal watchers have even called the consequent fallout as the worst crisis to hit the monarchy since Edward VIII's abdication in the 1930s, when the then-King fell in love with American divorcee Wallis Simpson but could not find family, political or public support to marry her.

By 1995 even Queen Elizabeth II had reportedly had enough of the tumultuous relationship – writing to Charles and Diana separately about seeking a divorce.

The year 1996 would see the divorce become final and Diana, though stripped of her styling as "Her Royal Highness," was permitted to continue residing at an apartment in Kensington Palace, and was reportedly given a handsome lump sum settlement of $22.5 million along with an annual $600,000 for her office. She had access to family assets like the jet and state apartments at St. James's Palace, and was even allowed to keep most of the jewelry from the marriage. As a member of the royal family and mother to the princes, she was still welcome to some state and public events. Most importantly, she and Charles had equal access to Princes William and Harry, who were at the time only 14 and 11 years of age, with whom they shared precious time when the boys were not in boarding school.

After the divorce, Princess Diana continued with her advocacies, most memorably walking through a minefield in Angola in January 1997, as part of the Red Cross' fight against the use of landmines. It was one more iconic image for a woman who had a lifetime of making them; she looked fearless and determined. Her courage and hard work are some of the reasons why she was so beloved and continues to be sorely missed, as that same year would put an end to her too-short life. By the end of August 1997, she was dead, killed in a tragic car accident in Paris with her new boyfriend, Dodi Fayed. Their intoxicated driver was trying to flee paparazzi.

Prince Charles, along with Diana's sisters, Sarah and Jane, retrieved her body from Paris and brought her back home, where a funeral fit for a royal and a beloved public figure was held before she was finally laid to rest in her family's storied Althorp estate. Her brother Earl Spencer, flanked by her two loving sons and they in turn flanked by their father Prince Charles and grandfather Prince Philip, famously walked behind her casket in the funeral procession. It was a heartbreaking sight.

As of this writing, Prince William is 35 years old, a few weeks shy of his 36th birthday, the age of his mother when she died. He is by now, alive for longer than he had his mum, who passed away when he was only 15. There is a lot of his life after Diana, but she would always be a part of it. From the obvious – like how he and his brother speak of her lovingly and openly and manage her public memory, and how the two princes made sure their respective fiancées would carry pieces of her jewelry – to the subtle but more fundamental, like how they continue her advocacies, champion open conversations on mental health issues, and how in particular, Prince William relates warily with the press and raises his family in a very hands-on way.

Prince William's Early Years

All of these would come later of course, as the two princes grew beneath the watchful eyes of the public as more or less well-adjusted and self-possessed young men. But during the time of their parents' tumultuous relationship, Prince William and Prince Harry struggled as many kids from broken families would have struggled – except magnified to the nth degree.

What other child, after all, would need to have a conversation with their mother about the restoration of a royal title? It will be recalled that part of the divorce entailed the stripping of Diana's "HRH." She was still "Diana, Princess of Wales," but the removal of "Her Royal Highness" – allegedly insisted upon by her ex-husband – meant she was required to curtsy to whoever still had the honorific, including her own sons. If rumors hold true, a young Prince William had once told her he would give her back the title when he became king.

The tumultuous years of Charles and Diana' trying relationship could not have been easy on their children, especially as William and Harry got older and became more exposed t it. After all, they had to juggle the concerns of normal children, like school and sports, o top of having to live up to the expectations foisted on them by their positions, growing up before the eyes of the world, and dealing with their family problems.

Prince William was a student at Mrs. Mynor's Nursery School in London from 1985 to 1987, and then at Weatherby School in Kensington from 1987-1990. At age 8, he would be sent to boarding school at Ludgrove Preparatory School, an institution which was at the time, almost 100 years old and previously attended by other aristocrats. He had bodyguards here, but was otherwise like the other kids in that he was to share a dorm room with other boys, use a communal bathroom, and keep to a schedule for meals, classes, prayers, and bedtime. Phone calls home were not allowed, and weekends spent outside campus were limited – tough restrictions for a boy of 8, even if he weren't His Royal Highness Prince William of Wales! The comprehensive education (covering a wide range of subjects including Art and French alongside Carpentry) came with trappings too though, with access to sports facilities including a pool and a nine-hole golf course.

Being away from school was tough, but in some ways, it offered stability as his parents' relationship deteriorated. Prince William stayed in Ludgrove from 1990 to 1995 – which were years of rapid decline for the marriage of Charles and Diana. In Ludgrove though, he had structure and a determined set of protectors, including some who reportedly shielded him from press coverage of his breaking family by keeping him away from the papers.

It was harder to protect him when he left Ludgrove for another storied institution, Eton College. It was hard enough for any new boy adjusting to a new and prestigious school, but Prince William also had to deal with his parents' scandalous relationship plastered across the front pages of the nation's papers. His years at Eton, from 1995 to 2000, would see some tough years for the royal family and especially for himself. Scandal after scandal included an alleged romance between his mother and rugby captain Will Carling, followed by Diana's Panorama interview in 1995. This was only on his first term. The Panorama interview was reportedly watched by the young Prince in the study of his housemaster and affected him deeply; as it would any child to hear their parents speak ill of each other or make their family problems known to others. But by 1996 there was the divorce and after that, his mother's shocking death in 1997.

It wasn't easy being Charles and Diana's son, but William's parents had their own shortcomings as individuals, apart from their conflicts with each other. Prince Charles, for example, was widely criticized for being an absentee parent in their earlier years, most notably after William had an accident in Ludgrove that necessitated a surgery to the head. Diana, for her part, while clearly a loving and passionate mother, suffered from mental issues that reportedly exposed her children to spells of tears, hysterics, and extreme moods. With their parents' busy schedules, the princes also spent much of their time with household staff, like their nannies. A particularly devoted one, Barbara Barnes, would make a lasting impression on William.

He called her "Baba" and she was a comfort to the rambunctious young royal, reading to him, sharing meals and giving him hugs.

Diana was rumored to be uncomfortable or even jealous of Barbara, who would eventually be let go for mysterious reasons. She would always be in William's heart, however, and she even got a coveted invitation to the Prince's wedding to Catherine Middleton 25 years later.

How any young man can come out of all the public and private drama with his sanity intact is a marvel. But to come out having excelled in school must be no less than a miracle. He was well-liked, excelled in sports and also good in academics. When Prince William left Eton in 2000, he was awarded A, B and C grades in his A-levels, Geography, History of Art and Biology, respectively. These, along with 10 GCSEs of eight As and two Bs, were said to put him amongst the brightest of the royal family.His schooling achievements showed promise of an intelligent future King. But at that time, his grades were great for another reason – they were good enough to secure him a spot at prestigious St. Andrew's University. There, he would be put in the path of a beautiful young woman who would forever change his life – that of Catherine Middleton, his future wife.

Prince William in Love

On the rugged shores of Scotland sits an intimate, medieval town called St. Andrews. Downtown is a simple affair of a few short streets and a Cathedral, but its environs are scenic and dramatic, with coastal views of jagged cliffs and crashing seas, golf courses, beaches, and centuries-old structures. There are picturesque streets and quaint shops, but also mansions and spired buildings. The town is home to a prestigious educational institution, St. Andrews University, that is considered one of the best not only in the United Kingdom but also in the world. Founded in 1413, it is the first Scottish university, but it also holds a more endearing distinction – it must be a wonderful place to fall in love.

The town is intimate and the student life diverse and thriving. In this coastal town, urban distractions are a distant reality (including paparazzi!). Friendships are formed and unique, unforgettable memories are made. If some estimates are to be believed, one in ten of its students marries a person they encountered while studying. Just ask, for example, the royal couple, Prince William and his wife, Duchess Catherine.

Before Kate

A man in line to inherit the British throne would have had his pick of the ladies even if he weren't as handsome or as personable as Prince William. But the son of Prince Charles and Princess Diana has a list of conquests that is both relatively short and generally has little-verified information.

Jessica "Jecca" Craig, a stunning, strong-willed brunette, is said to have captured the Prince's heart when they were teenagers. The Craigs moved in fancy environmentalist circles, and her father, Ian Craig, who owned a ranch in Kenya, was good friends with the late brother of Prince Charles' beloved Camilla. They were family friends, and Prince William spent some time at the family's Kenyan ranch during his gap year. Whether or not they really dated or for how seriously is unverified. What is apparent is that they remain friendly, and William would go on to attend her brother's wedding in 2008, she would be a presence in his and Kate's in 2011, they set tongues wagging when they hunted wild boar and stag with friends in Spain in 2014, and he flew all the way from the UK to attend Jecca's own wedding in Kenya in 2016.

Prince William and childhood friend Rose Farquhar, daughter of former Master of the Beaufort Hunt, Captain Ian Farquhar, dated briefly in the year 2000. The aspiring singer and actress would later on appear in TV talent shows like *How Do You Solve a Problem Like Maria?*, a 2006 search for an actress to play Maria in *The Sound of Music* on West End; and singing competition, *The Voice* in 2016. Her resume also includes the pursuit of her craft at the prestigious Lee Strasberg Institute in New York. There are no publicly available details on this failed romance, but one of the things many royal watchers can agree on, is that Ms. Farquhar has similar looks to the woman Prince William would eventually marry.

Arabella Musgrave, whom the Prince had also known since they were little, really caught his eye in the summer of 2001, just before he headed for St. Andrew's. They danced and drank and had a passionate romance that cooled down as Prince William had to leave for university. For a time, it was reported that they saw each other whenever he returned. As part of the "Glosse Posse-" close friends of the Prince from Gloucestershire - the glamorous PR exec of Gucci would be in attendance at the Prince's wedding to Catherine Middleton in 2011.

The Prince's first semester at St. Andrews saw him dating Carley Massy-Birch, a self-confessed country bumpkin. It was a trait that appealed to the Prince, who had a love for the countryside. It probably did not hurt that Carley had what many remember to be a legendary derrière. They had a short-lived romance that allegedly ended due to the Prince's continued links with Arabella Musgrave. The relationship was so low-key it would not be known publicly until years after they graduated.

Olivia Hunt was also early in capturing Prince William's heart while he was at St. Andrew's, but she was quickly out of the picture when Kate Middleton came sashaying down the runway at a charity fashion show and made an impression on the Prince in her see-through dress. Olivia, a writer, reportedly remains friends with the couple and they have even gone skiing together. They move in the same circles and when she married one of the UK's "hottest" barristers, Nicholas Wilkinson, in 2016, Prince Harry and a number of their common friends were in attendance. She also attended Pippa Middleton's wedding in 2017.

The blue-blooded actress, heiress, and socialite, Isabella Calthorpe, has an impressive pedigree via parents John Anstruther-Gough-Calthorpe and Lady Mary-Gaye Georgiana Lorna Curzon. She could have been a more traditional match for Prince William... even if one didn't see the slight resemblance she had with the Prince's stunning mother, Diana. She and the Prince reportedly met at a dinner party in 2001 and chatted the night away at a ball in 2004 or 2005, but wouldn't be seriously linked to each other until William and Kate's brief separation later. The romance wouldn't get very far – the Prince's affections were not returned, if accounts are true! - and Isabella eventually married billionaire Sir Richard Branson's son, Sam, in 2013.

The above list shows a friend who might have been more, puppy love, the passionate summer romance, the quiet country secret, the one the Prince let go, and the one who would do the same to him. But as one of the world's most eligible bachelors, Prince William would be romantically linked with other women to varying degrees. There's Davina Duckworth-Chad, who joined him, his friends and family in an Aegean cruise in 1999. Rumors of flirtations and brief relationships would be in the news too, such as with equestrienne Rosie van Cutsem and security consultant Natalie Hicks-Lobbecke. There would be petite blonde Tess Shepherd too, with whom the Prince reportedly shared a drunken, dancefloor embrace at London hotspot Boujis.

But for all of these women's bloodlines, impressive names and royal connections, the Prince's heart would eventually be claimed by his university roommate, Kate Middleton – daughter of former airline employees turned party supply millionaires, and whose mother's side was in the working class, including a store clerk, builders, laborers and coal miners. "Commoner Kate," sneered some. "New Money," said others. But by her grace and poise, she would make her own way forward as one-half of the world's most watched and beloved couples.

Catherine Middleton

Catherine Elizabeth Middleton is the eldest of Michael and Carole Middleton's three children. She was born on the 9th of January, 1982, in Reading, Berkshire, England. At the time of her birth, her parents were airline employees. When she was two years old, the family moved to Amman, Jordan, where they lived for two and a half years as her father worked. She attended nursery school there when she turned three. They returned to Berkshire in 1986, and soon afterwards she enrolled at co-educational St. Andrew's School in Pangbourne.

The family would undergo a major change in 1987, when her parents founded Party Pieces, a mail order company supplying party paraphernalia. The company's success would turn the couple into multi-millionaires, with recent estimates pegging a value of $50 million on the thriving business. Kate and her younger siblings, Pippa (born in 1984) and James (born in 1987), would consequently have a comfortable life and excellent opportunities in schooling.

Kate was a student at St. Andrew's School until 1995, and she would later describe her time there as amongst the happiest years of her life. She discovered a love and talent for sport here, and by one of her teacher's accounts, held a long-standing record at the high jump that would only be broken after 20 years. One of the most famous stories to come out about Kate Middleton during her time in St. Andrew's School is that she was involved in public speaking and drama. A video surfaced of her as a young girl in a school play, portraying a character who is told by a fortune teller that she would marry a prince – which as the world knows, would one day come true!

After the happy time she spent at St. Andrew's School, she would get a bit of a shock at the next place she enrolled in. Kate spent a brief time at all-girls school Downe House, where she reportedly was either a victim of intense bullying or was someone who simply did not find it the right fit. Either way, she stayed all of two terms before being moved away at age 14. Rumors of her ever having been bullied were never confirmed, but she gave royal watchers something to read into when she and Prince William included the charity, Beatbullying, in a list of charities wedding guests and other well-wishers could donate to in lieu of gifts to them on their special day. Even after their marriage, she and Prince William would continue to be an advocate for victims of bullying.

Following her rough time at Downe House, she attended co-educational Marlborough College in Wiltshire, where she remained until the year 2000. It's a prestigious institution too, counting Princess Eugenie as one of its alumni. While there, Kate showed athletic prowess and participated in sports like hockey, netball, and tennis. She also studied A-level Chemistry, Biology and Art. She would eventually pass 11 GCSEs and 3 A-level exams, marks that would allow her into a prestigious institution like St. Andrew's University in Scotland, where she would eventually find her Prince Charming.

From Friend to Future Queen

Before enrolling at St. Andrew's University in Scotland, Kate Middleton had a stimulating gap year, with stints in the British Institute in Florence and spending time in Chile with British charity Raleigh International, among other pursuits. Prince William had his own gap year adventures. He spent time in Kenya (and time getting closer to Jecca Craig, if rumors are to be believed), and was also in Latin America with Raleigh International. His travels and volunteer work had him doing a variety of tasks, including building a playground in Chile, painting homes, and milking cows on an English farm. His busy schedule wouldn't let his social life suffer, however; he'd reportedly had time to date Arabella Musgrave before heading off to university.

Prince William and Catherine Middleton missed each other in Chile only by a few weeks. They were tossed in different places in the world and cavorting with different people, but inevitably, their paths were slowly winding their way toward each other.

St. Andrew's University, as had been previously described, seems like a great place to live, learn and fall in love. Prince William's time there would give him unprecedented freedom to do just these things, especially because the small town was not only far from the hustle, bustle and easy press access of a big city, but arrangements were also made with the media to generally have respect for the young prince's privacy during his education. This allowed the young prince a lot of space for pursuing as much of a "normal life" as a man of his stature could ever hope to have. Over his time there, the small town, with its population of less than 20,000 people, generally left him alone to do ordinary things like walking in the streets or shopping at the grocery store.

Prince William's schooling in St. Andrew's is a break from royal tradition; 150 years of history would see royal families in either Oxford or Cambridge, including William's father Charles, uncle Edward, and great-grandfather King George VI. Though it was lovely at St. Andrew's and he found friends (and dates like the quiet suppers he is said to have shared with Carley Massy-Birch) fairly easily, the university he ultimately chose for himself was 50 miles up from Edinburgh and could be confining and stark to someone used to an entirely different life. William was a long way from home and missed his friends, the London nightlife, and, if reports are to be believed, the company of Arabella Musgrave, too. He was homesick, on top of allegedly finding the coursework at St. Andrew's challenging. The Prince discussed his misgivings with his understanding father, Prince Charles, and the school worked with them to help adjust. From his art history major he switched to Geography, and eventually settled in much better.

His friendships would play no small part in that, including a kinship he found with athletic, pretty and shy Kate Middleton, whom he would often run into at St. Salvator's, one of the residence halls in the university. She shared his first major, and though he would eventually deviate from this, they had many other similar interests and plenty of opportunities to know each other better. They shared healthy meals at the dining hall with their other friends, and enjoyed sports like swimming and skiing.

Other than meeting in school, and details of the shy future duchess blushing and 'scuttling off,' the precise circumstances of their meeting are unknown. A biography of Kate, citing sources from her time in Marlborough, would later claim the couple were actually introduced by common friend earlier than when they were at St. Andrew's While that information is not confirmed, some quarters have pointed out how Kate made a surprising shift from her original plans of enrolling at Edinburgh University, said to be her first choice, to deciding on St. Andrew's. The information fits into the narrative pushed by some people that

Catherine Middleton is more calculating than she would have the public believe, but this is just one mystery the rest of us would simply have to live with, at least for now.

At any rate, there are relatively few secrets between this couple and the public, and much more is known about how their love story unfolded after that fateful first meeting (whenever or wherever that might have actually been).

Prince William kept a low-key and some might even say, a rather boring life in St. Andrews. He would swim and go cycling, and made the occasional appearance at the student union to play pool. He spent time with his friends and immersed in school activities, one of which would prove a turning point in his life. It was March 2002, and he wouldn't be looking at his friend Kate Middleton the same way again.

Kate was a known beauty, deemed amongst the prettiest in "Sally's," as their St. Salvator's residence is known. She and William had been friends for some time, but on one evening in March 2002, at the yearly Don't Walk fashion show for charity, she took the runway in black underwear beneath a see-through dress. The Prince was in the front row and he, like everyone else, knew she looked "hot."

A witness who was present at a post-show after-party would later claim that the Prince made a move that very night. He appeared to have leaned in for a kiss, which was dodged cleanly by the woman who would one day be his wife and Duchess. She was said to be dating someone else at the time, a fourth-year student named Rupert Finch. She may have also wanted to play it cool, and give an otherwise privileged prince a little bit more to work for.

Either way, whether or not Kate Middleton had intended to do so, it seemed as if she had snagged herself a Prince.

 At the beginning of Prince William's second year, in 2002, he moved out of the campus residence halls in favor of living in an apartment with his friends. He roomed in with Kate and their pals, Olivia Bleasdale and his fellow former Etonian, Fergus Boyd.

Moving into the centrally-located 13a Hope Street offered Prince William a shot at a normal college life. They paid rent. They cleaned and shopped for groceries at the local Tesco, and they hosted dinner parties. Perfectly ordinary - except of course, with bomb-proof doors, bullet-proof windows, and a complex laser security system. Absolutely normal too, for a student like him to find and nurture a university love – except of course, that he and Kate had to keep their growing relationship a closely guarded secret.

It wouldn't last for very long and soon, their secret became an "open secret" in the university. In a bid for more privacy, the couple moved away from the city center to Balgove House, a property owned by the prince's distant cousin, Henry Cheape. The four-bedroom cottage sat on a private estate that was large enough to have outbuildings that could house the Prince's security officers, as well as to have sprawling, walled grounds that allowed the couple to enjoy picnics and long, romantic walks.

But the secret that became an open secret would cease to be a secret of any kind by the first quarter of 2004, during a ski trip to the Klosters in Switzerland. Photos of William and Kate were splashed across the papers, visual confirmation of the rumors long circulating that the Prince was in a serious relationship. The Prince had a girlfriend, and the scoop was too delicious for the press to seriously keep to the agreement they had with the Palace regarding the Prince's privacy while at university. Suddenly everyone wanted to know about Kate.

Prince William was aware of what dating him could mean for a girl. In an interview, he talked about how his dating someone could put that person in an awkward situation, and he was right. Kate Middleton would hold that awkward position for a lon time, but it was one of the ways that she shined. She was polite and discreet, and had a family who was just as careful. She kept a cool head and kept herself grounded, even a attention on their relationship intensified.

As a modern couple of extraordinary mean they had a lot of opportunities to get to know each other better outside of university too. Getaways included Kate accompanying William to Balmoral, Highgrove, and Sandringham for hunting seasons, sometimes with friends and other times wit Kate's siblings, Pippa and James. Aside from hunting, they enjoyed activities like cooking taking long walks in the moors or just enjoying being together before a roaring log fire.

But the Prince seemed to need more than quiet country sojourns in his life as an in-demand young royal. He had a rather outgoing group of friends too, and enjoyed the occasional gregarious activity. By mid-2004 he was reportedly getting restless in St. Andrew's, and his relationship with Kate was experiencing some strain. Finals were coming too and soon after that, graduation and the end of the quiet life they've crafted in the small town that was home for their years of studying. Questions remained on how the couple would navigate life outside of university, moving forward.

Some time apart seemed to be in order to clarify things. William, along with some friends, planned an all-boys sailing vacation to Greece. Among these friends were the controversial but loyal Guy Pelly, whom Kate allegedly did not completely approve of (he would eventually be a valued ally, and was close enough to the couple to be a rumored godparent to their son, Prince George). She wouldn't be alone in this assessment, if she did think it of him at the time. Mr. Pelly, whom the press have called a party animal and was known as the "court jester" of their illustrious group, seemed to have a talent for fun. He ran some of London's hottest nightclubs, a talent he may have honed when he, along with the Princes William and Harry, allegedly had wild, private, drunken get-togethers with their friends. During William's planned Greek holiday, Kate spent part of the summer with her family in Berkshire and part of it in France, where she reportedly confided to friends of their relationship issues. William, if rumors are to be believed, wasn't just longing for his old social whirlwind, he was also somewhat interested in other women, perhaps Jecca Craig and/or Isabella Calthorpe.

It was still Kate, however, who would be spending time with William's family during Prince Charles' birthday, and on the holiday to Klosters just before Prince Charles married his beloved Camilla in a civil ceremony. And when the young couple finally graduated from St. Andrew's University in 2005, it was still Kate that William would spend his free time with before setting off for the Royal Military Academy at Sandhurst.

By 2006, they would be photographed kissing in public for the first time, again while on a skiing holiday. As they went on more travels and public events, and would be seen together when William wasn't away in training, the seriousness of the relationship was clear to many. There was talk of the couple going down the aisle soon – but not quite, from William's mouth.

Will They or Won't They?

One of Kate Middleton's most important public appearances before their marriage was when she and her parents, who had also become close to the Prince, were invited to attend William's 2006 graduation ceremony at Sandhurst. Quite an honor, considering the Prince had also invited his grandmother the Queen, and his dad Prince Charles and wife Camilla, the Duchess of Cornwall. The bets were on – a royal engagement must be in the cards, and soon.

In the meantime, Kate Middleton suffered the rigors of being a public persona, with none of the perks and only the barest of protections. She was given advice on how to handle the media, had some support from a press team, and the occasional protection officer. She handled things well even when she was swamped by photographers, and was always a cool customer with great, accessible style. If rumors are to be believed, sometimes she was even more cautious of public appearances than Prince William - she reportedly had to remind him of how to conduct himself when out with friends, and had reportedly even taken it upon herself to ensure their privacy when going out. No matter how poised she was in public though there was still no escaping the fact that Prince William had been right about placing his women in awkward positions – after all, what could a princess-in-waiting do, at the strange place between being a 'commoner' and the future King's wife?

Like Princess Diana before her, Kate was hounded by the press and sometimes ridiculed by the public, not excluding some classists in high English circles. Were she and her sister Pippa social climbers desperate to marry up? Was she lazy, or a gold-digger? How long does 'Waity Katie' really have to wait?

Much longer, as it turned out, for 2007 would give the couple and those rooting for them a scare. The couple was spending less time together, either because of William's commitments to his training, or by his preference to spend time with family and friends. There would be nights clubbing in London, with stories and sometimes photos to match that would prove hurtful and embarrassing to his girlfriend. By April 2007, the couple called it quits.

But Kate Middleton was a tough cookie and a smart woman. She gave William space and kept her quiet poise, but knew she would be photographed so she let her pictures speak a thousand words. She slipped on more chic clothing, went out more with her equally gorgeous sister Pippa, and showed the Prince just what he was missing. She also looked after herself well, and joined a group training for a charity dragon boat row. The sport gave her both ease of mind and a well-toned body. She was keeping busy and so was William, but behind the scenes, they were in contact and on the mend.

In just a few months the couple reunited, and for the next years went on as they always have – traveling, holidaying with each other's families and attending public events together. Amongst these key appearances were at William's graduation from the R.A.F in April 2008, and at the Garter ceremony later that year in June. Over the years, they found whatever time they could within the demands of their respective careers to be together; he was pursuing his military aspirations while Kate worked as an accessories buyer for the fashion brand, Jigsaw. She also did some work for the Middletons' party supplies business. But this wouldn't last for very long, as the couple would be engaged by October 2010.

William proposed while on a romantic holiday in Kenya, with a familiar blue stunner of a ring. The oval sapphire was surrounded by 14 solitaire diamonds, clocking in at 12-carats. The Garrard piece was previously owned by the groom-to-be's iconic mother, Princess Diana. After almost a decade of friendship and a pressure-cooker situation of a relationship, 'Waity Katie' was waiting no more, and Prince Charming was going to be her husband.

On April 29, 2011, the couple wed in a lavish ceremony watched by billions all over the world. On the occasion of his wedding, the Queen conferred on her grandson the title William, Duke of Cambridge. Kate

Middleton would thereafter be the Duchess of Cambridge – a fantastic departure from 'Waity Katie' indeed!

But William's life was that of unceasing pressure, and soon, attention would turn away from finding a bride, to making an heir. The perfect royal couple wouldn't disappoint on this score for very long, though. By late 2012, the official announcement of their first pregnancy is made, and George Alexander Louis – formally known as His Royal Highness Prince George of Cambridge - would be born months later in July 2013. He would be joined by a sister, Princess Charlotte Elizabeth Diana in May 2015, as well as a baby brother by April 2018.

By many accounts, William is a good father and a very hands-on one. He speaks openly of his love for their children and can be affectionate to them even in public. He is often seen carrying them in his arms or holding hands with them, and has confessed to fatherhood making him more emotional than he used to be. He is said to be determined to give his family stability and protection – and had even succeeded in petitioning for a no-fly zone over their home, Amner Hall, in Norfolk.

Not quite the concerns of a normal parent, but like any other mom and dad, Prince William had more conventional struggles too. A single father who snagged a chat with the Duchess of Cambridge at a charity event later revealed that Kate told him Prince William struggled early on too. The world got a peek of something like this firsthand in 2018, during a church service for Anzac Day. The event was held just a few days after Catherine gave birth to their third child, and William was caught on video struggling to stay awake. Many in the public took this to be symptomatic of life with a newborn baby and happily aired their support for the sleep deprived dad of three!

A Life in Public Service

In unsubtle ways, being a royal was a literal job with financial contributions to the larger economy just by their very existence. They keep the wheels turning across industries and keep businesses running even by just the very content of their lives. They also promote their country outside of it, with effects on tourism and spending. William's role as bachelor prince, romantic Romeo and eventually, doting dad certainly fill the pages of papers and websites, feed TV ratings, spur tourism and sell merchandise. But existing alone is not enough. Royals can't just live their lives and expect to thus contribute. They need to be visible, they need to be accessible, and they are still expected to do some actual work, leveraging their public personas to push their advocacies and promote their charities, all while appearing to be politically neutral. There are sometimes very thin lines between these.

The extremely important visibility and work aspects of being a royal have been problematic when it comes to the otherwise uncontroversial Prince William. Indeed, other than the short-lived troubles he and Kate Middleton struggled with before getting engaged, he was sometimes considered boring, press-averse and work-shy. With a life settled with his Duchess and beloved family, then, what can we make of the Prince's other pursuits as a working royal?

Prince William had started university with an interest in the history of art, before finishing with geography. He then headed for military training, just like his brother Prince Harry. These are very diverse interests with differing paths, on top of his duties as a royal. So how does a talented man with plenty of prospects and privileges juggle all of these toward a career?

His time with the military showed him taking part in some very interesting operations. On the HMS *Iron Duke*, he participated in a multi-million-pound drug bust, seizing cocaine in the Caribbean Sea. He enjoyed flying too, and for a time was with the R.A.F. as a search-and-rescue pilot. At the time, in 2008, some in the press speculated his focus on his military career were just attempts to delay his official royal duties rather than serious pursuits. They certainly contributed to delays in his marriage to Kate, too.

Whether or not this was true cannot be proven. What seems clear though, is that William's romantic style and career focus shows a man who is headstrong and perhaps in his own way, also wise. Marriage and taking on official royal duties would have made any semblance of a "normal" life pretty much out of reach forever afterwards, why not give it more of a try? Besides, he has also seen how marrying so young could have been detrimental to his mom, so why not sow some wild oats, as the saying goes? As for career, what real rush was there to end his personal pursuits and trade them in for official duties? He was still behind his father, Prince Charles, in line to the throne – and

Charles himself had in some ways been adrift, spending most of his life trying to be useful while he waited for his own ascension. Why not nourish a career if he would just be standing in line behind the long-lived Windsors?

Taking Flight

Prince William would serve almost eight years in the military. When he was a Royal Air Force pilot involved in Search and Rescue, he was known to comrades as "Flight Lt. Wales." His position did not allow him to be involved in the riskiest of roles (his brother Harry, for example, would be allowed to do tours in Afghanistan), but he was well-liked, conducted himself professionally, and as a pilot, had direct contributions to saving lives, often in rough conditions. He left the military in 2013 shortly after the birth of his first son, George, but took on employment in the private sector in 2014 as a pilot for an air ambulance company (his salary was reportedly donated to charity).

For a while, he juggled fatherhood with work on top of his royal duties, until he ended his stint as a helicopter pilot for air ambulance services in 2017, so that he may finally devote himself fully to his royal duties and advocacies.

Work-Shy William?

William's seeming lack of commitment to his royal duties has been an issue for some time

It must be remembered that his grandparents, Queen Elizabeth and her royal consort Prince Philip, have the constitution to continue working heavily even into their 90s. Over his royal life, for example, Prince Philip would go on to attend tens of thousands of engagements by the time he retired – at age 96!

A critical press isn't afraid to let the young Prince have it and some of them were bold enough to keep count and show receipts. One paper alleged the royal's first official engagement of 2016 was 47 days deep into the year, and even then it was a damaging one. At the height of the Brexit issue, a speech made by the Prince before the Foreign Office was construed as Pro-EU, which would have been a break from the royal's neutrality when it came to politics

(Kensington Palace thereafter denied it was a Pro-EU stand).

But it wasn't just the ruckus caused by the wording of his speech that was problematic to some royal watchers. At the time, his grandfather, over 94 years old at the time, was doing over 100 more engagements than he was. In one year, his public job count at home was 87 and 35 abroad, while in comparison, his grandfather was coming it at 250 and the Queen got up to as high as 341. In early 2017, he even missed Commonwealth Day services to go skiing and partying with friends. He had a job at the time as a pilot of course, and was a relatively new dad besides. But rumors were also swirling that he was a reluctant royal with more interest in being a gentleman farmer in the country or hanging out with his friends than carrying out his duties.

Prince William, who is a conservationist active in anti-poaching organizations, would also draw flak for advocating wildlife preservation while being an avid hunter (albeit of non-endangered and non-protected species).

In short, not only has he been doing little compared to others in his royal family, what he was doing was also not accomplished very well.

Certain members of the press had another axe to grind, too. Was the Prince being overly restrictive with media coverage of his family? Was he overstepping bounds in his attempts to control their coverage? The no-fly zone over their home earlier mentioned is just one manifestation of William's protective streak. They've limited press presence in certain events, not even bothering to distinguish tabloids from more reputable outlets. His staff is also known to be relentless with their complaints to and of the press, and the Prince has never been shy about his wariness of the media.

The Prince had always been open with his discomfort and distrust, but then again, why wouldn't he feel that way? To say that he has an understandable reserve would be an understatement. He saw his mother brought to tears by the press' constant attention, and their relentless pursuit had ultimately somehow contributed to her tragic death. He saw how getting a scoop could cause profound embarrassment and ridicule to his parents, and there was little he could do when the media gave his own future wife trouble while they were dating and she had no official designation or protection. His friends have been targeted too, and sometimes elaborately; there are reports of one of them being lured with a ruse on a business meeting that ended up with one of the attendees wired, and asking questions about William. Aggressive tactics directed at his children have been known too, with some behaviors bordering on stalking. Of course Prince William is going to be cautious.

The World Will Keep Watching

In a candid interview about accusations that he was work-shy, Prince William responded by saying he looked at his grandmother the

Queen as a role model for duty, and that he would eagerly take on tasks when they are given to him. He also seemed to have a good attitude about criticisms sent his way, saying he couldn't completely ignore them, nor does he take them "completely to heart."

For a man who can expect eyes to always be turned his way, and consequently an inability to please everyone – this actually seems to be a healthy way of looking at the world. He is a bright man and a circumspect one, who appears to give thought to his decisions and the ability to stick to them.

He saw by his mother's example that marrying young was hard; he sowed his wild oats and did things on his own time. He saw that royal roles could be restrictive, so he sought out ways to experience a "normal life and pursue a career before committing himself to official duties. He had a rocky childhood, so he is doing his best to provide stability and protection for his own family.

Prince William has shown an ability to learn hard lessons and make careful moves from them. In some ways, he is "new" to a purely royal role. In some ways, he is "new" to his role as head of his own family. He might make early mistakes and bad moves. He may look work-shy and press-averse. But eventually, he is likely to find his stride. He is likely to find a way to balance understandable concerns for his family's safety and privacy, but also their need to be in the public eye in order to be effective at their job as royals. His history shows he can learn and find ways to grow and compromise, and settle into his roles be it as a student, a son, a husband, a father or, eventually, a King.

In the meantime, he *is* working.

He is a staunch protector of his mother's memory and legacy. In 2007, ten years after her death, William worked with his brother Prince Harry in a concert to raise funds for Princess Diana's charities. They've also participated in documentaries about her, often sharing very heartfelt and intimate details about what their mother was like in private, and their struggles with grief. The Prince is patron to many charities, and had always credited his family as heavy influencers in his sense of duty and responsibility. Amongst his causes are Centrepoint, which is focused on homeless youth; and the Tusk Trust, which works for wildlife preservation in Africa. Along with his brother, he established The Royal Foundation of the Duke and Duchess of Cambridge and Prince Harry, a vehicle for launching a variety of projects or increasing the impact and reach of existing projects and organizations that fit into their criteria, including the famous Invictus Games for wounded, ill and injured servicemen all over the world; the Heads Together Campaign, which advocates better approaches to mental health and fundraising for mental health initiatives; and a Cyberbullying taskforce. This is just a small slice of the kind of charity work that Prince William does. He is involved to varying degrees in many other causes, including wildlife conservation, AIDS & HIV, Cancer, Education, and Grief Support. Like his father, Prince William has also taken to writing to government ministers, though not so much on behalf of a cause or to lobby a position (which would have been against the royal family's usual neutrality) but to connect charities to people in government.

Yes, Prince William is working.

And as always, the world is watching closely.

Prince Harry

A Prince Harry Biography

Katy Holborn

Introduction

Thank you for choosing this book. In it we will look at the life of a young royal who has helped to bring the monarchy into the 21st century.

As a central part of the slimmed down House of Windsor that his father, Prince Charles, has brought about, Harry is a man for today.

Along with his brother and sister in law, Prince William and the Duchess of Cambridge, he is the face of a monarchy for the twenty-first century.

A man who is determined to combine living his own life with public duty. Who is keen to develop his own relationships as privately as possible, while doing immeasurable amounts of good for the country – and world – as a whole.

Harry is a man who fought bravely in Afghanistan, who never lost the affection of the public despite being embroiled in some controversial events.

A man for whom the death of his mother, in the most unbelievable of circumstances, would shape his life.

Harry was a troubled teen and twenty something until, in his late twenties, he began to realize that he must face up to her death and by doing so, could use his own experiences to do wonders for others.

Today Prince Harry appears to be on the edge of marriage, a man doing good for many others, whose own life is finally taking a turn for the best.

He is the approachable, take me as you find me, member of the royal family, in some ways very like his grandfather, Prince Philip.

Whether he is meting out tough justice for intrusive members of the paparazzi or helping African children hit by the horror of HIV, Harry is the royal for whom we all hold affection.

This is his story.

Chapter One – The Invictus Games

For most of us, it is hard to imagine living with no legs, or one arm, or an injury so horrific that death seems more of a reward than a threat.

But in September 2017 five hundred and fifty women and men lined up for the third Invictus Games, every single one of them seriously injured or ill and made so by their contribution towards settling the world's conflicts.

There are many events for war heroes around the world, possibly the biggest, and one with the highest profile is Prince Harry's own contribution – the Invictus Games.

Four of these heroes who would represent Britain in the Invictus Games appeared in a

BBC Documentary called 'Invictus Games – Battle to the Start Line.' They have stories that, prior to the creation of these games, would not have been told.

Bernie was in the Guards, and a prouder man would be harder to imagine. His dining room is called the Mess and has been turned into a celebration of his achievements.

Pictures, bearskins, a photograph of the Queen – the walls and shelf spaces are covered with memories. Bernie is a big, hearty bloke, clearly a man's man. His pride at showing off the 'mess' is tear-jerkingly clear on his face.

Bernie was in a vehicle in Afghanistan that was blown up by an improvised device. He lost his legs. His life changed in that one split second.

His wife describes a man returning home who had become 'hollow'; somebody who looks the same but whose inner self, his soul perhaps, had been blown away along with his legs.

She movingly describes how she began to dislike the shell of the man she still, very much, loved.

Bernie describes how his anger grew on his return to Britain. He would seethe at seeing a person jogging, that emotion turning to hate, because it was something he could not do himself.

For a man such as this, it is the pride of being selected to represent his country at the Invictus Games that has allowed his true soul to re-enter his body.

'I'm glad he's back,' says his wife.

Michele took nine years to reach the status of Para-medic in the forces. She tells of how her PTSD (Post-traumatic stress disorder) ruined her life.

Trying to cope with the trauma of being sent, nonstop, to the worst incidents in the Helmand region of Afghanistan took its toll. Seeing six children blown up by an improvised explosive device stuck in her head in particular.

Back home, life hit rock bottom. Her fiancé left her, unable to cope with her mental state. She was heavily depressed. She became suicidal.

Then an email came through, inviting her to take part in the games. Not seeing herself as good at sports, she deleted it. But the email came twice more, and it was enough to give Michele the preparedness to give it a go.

That interest has transformed her back into a woman with a purpose.

Scott describes being blown up, also by an IED. He is left on the road, waiting for help. The chin strap from his helmet is strangling him.

So sure is he that death is inevitable, that he runs through in his head that everything back at home is covered, and then waits for blackness.

Now Scott once more has a purpose – taking part in the games has lifted his spirit, given him a reason for carrying on.

For Jack, the pride of being invited to take part in the Invictus Games comes from the chance to wear the Union Jack once more on his chest.

The Invictus Games are the brainchild of Prince Harry. Himself a former soldier, himself a man who has suffered tragedy in his life.

But also, a man with the position and the power to do something positive for others.

Harry set up the Invictus Games because he saw sport as a route through which both the physical and emotional damage to those involved in conflict could be addressed. Not cured, but healed.

For Harry, one of the surprising benefits of his idea has been the impact seeing the soldiers compete has had on the general public.

He had not foreseen how the games would raise both the profile, but also the support, for soldiers who have suffered so greatly in the line of duty.

Rather than becoming hidden away, in all honesty, a bit of an embarrassment, they have become celebrated for their bravery.

No longer, as was the case with Vietnam and, to some extent, the Falklands conflict, would these victims be cast into the shadows.

Harry points out that it is not just the wounded themselves who have suffered, but their families and friends. And the psychological benefits of preparing for and taking part in the games has been of help to those family members as well.

When Jack got the news of his inclusion in the games, the joy on the faces of his parents matched that on his own, as they bent down to hug him in his wheelchair.

And for Bernie, who is made Captain of the ninety-strong squad from Britain, he is back. He can never be the physical man he was before, but he has regained self-respect, belief in himself.

The first games took place in 2014. The plan was always that they would become a regular event. However, nobody would be sure how they would be received.

Having a Prince on board gave them a public interest that would help, but the Foundation behind the games were still overwhelmed by the bids that came in.

Following on from London, the second games were held in Florida, then in 2017, Toronto took over as hosts.

In 2018 Sydney will become the venue for the fourth games.

Behind the event is the desire that those who have been injured will remain defined by their spirit and personality, not by their injuries.

The word 'Invictus' means unconquered. These are women and men who will not be conquered by their physical and mental wounds but who will fight against them, and win.

Prince Harry says about the games 'They have been about teammates choosing to cross the line together.

Not wanting to come second, but not wanting the other guys to either. These games have shown the very best of human spirit.'

The games allow the power of sport to be channeled into good. But they are not just about sporting competition, they are about the power to harness the heart, challenge the mind and bring about change for good.

Competitors will cheer on the last over the line, rather than embark on their own celebrations. They are likely to engage in crossing the finishing line together, a team once more.

If being a Prince, and a senior member of the Royal Family means having the opportunity of changing lives for the better, then that is something that the youngest son of the heir to the throne has embraced.

Completely and utterly.

Chapter Two – A Prince is Born

Perhaps a better title for this chapter should be 'Another Prince is Born' because Harry is, of course, the younger of two princes.

Nowadays, he is slipping down the line of those who might inherit the throne, as his older brother William's family grows. At birth, he was in third position.

So, although it is unlikely that he will ever become king, he is nevertheless very active as a royal.

Harry was born on September 15th 1984. As had been the case with William, the pregnancy was difficult for his mother, with bad morning sickness a feature.

And being third in line to the throne did not equate to a trouble-free childhood. We will look later in this book at his relationship with his parents.

But it is fair to say that this was very close with both. Yet it was also tough, as regular heated arguments between Prince Charles and Princess Diana were eventually followed by their unofficial separation.

That soon became official and divorce came next. The untimely death of his mother had an expectedly serious impact on his life. One that would take years with which to come to terms.

But that is later. From being a very young child, Harry was a mixture of livewire and the reticent. He had a love for the outdoors, for sports and arts. He took up riding and hunting as soon as he was able.

Home was Kensington Palace during the week, but weekends would be spent in Gloucestershire, and Highgrove House. There, both Harry and his older brother would await their father's arrival, usually by helicopter, from whatever business he had been involved with during the day.

They would rush to him even while the rotors roared. Harry was equally close to Diana. In a way, even closer.

It was Diana who was particularly determined that Harry and William would have as normal a childhood as possible.

And his father was determined that the boys would not suffer from the unhappiness he had endured as a child himself.

That unhappiness had originated from the sense of duty over family that his parents shared. This was more a mark on the times than any unthinking behavior.

Although he had been very close to his grandmother, the Queen Mother, and one of h nannies when Charles was sent to boarding school life deteriorated.

It was bad enough in Cheam, relatively close to home in Berkshire. But forced into the harsh regime that dominated at his father's alma mater, Gordonstoun, had been a nightmare for the young Charles.

He was certain that his own children's lives would fare better.

Diana took her sons on trips to Macdonald's, the zoo and to theme parks. As far as is possible considering their background and future import (William would one day be king) Diana and Charles would ensure that their offspring experienced that which other children of their age went through.

Life was fun. Bath time would feature endless bubbles crashing onto the floor, and races through the polished corridors of Kensington Palace.

When schooling began, Harry first attended Mrs. Mynors' Nursery in Notting Hill. This was a school that followed the Montessori methods, something with which Harry' mother was familiar.

She had worked as an assistant at such a school when courting Charles. Montessori schools follow principles of hands-on, child centered education.

They often produce children with strengths in creativity and the arts.

In 1989 Harry started school proper, joining Wetherby School where his brother was already a pupil.

Harry's early years were tricky at Wetherby. He had troubles mixing with some of the other children, but after having parts in two Christmas plays (in which all children would have taken part) he settled steadily.

Particularly enjoyable in his activities remained sport and arts.

Traditionally, heirs to the throne had been home tutored through their early school years. Prince Charles broke that pattern, attending Hil House School in London before heading to Cheam in Berkshire.

Both young Princes followed this change. After Wetherby School, each attended Ludgrove. This is also in Buckinghamshire, but is situated much closer to their main London home than Cheam.

Ludgrove is an all boys' full boarding school. It is hidden away behind Wokingham, close to a small railway station.

Security and privacy were issues for both Princes, especially from the paparazzi who seemed to want daily tales of the boys and, even more so, their mother.

But Charles and Diana were determined that school days would be a chance for their children to be out of the limelight. It might, after all, be the only times in their lives when that could be achieved.

Ludgrove School was ideal. Entry is down a long driveway. The impression a visitor would get is that they have taken the wrong turning, as the drive passes beyond pig fields and other farmland.

Then, a couple of buildings are encountered. Included here are some modern constructions which were built to house security staff for the Princes.

They are now lived in by teachers working at the school. Finally, the main entrance appears on the left.

A large, but not especially grand, house marks the home of the Headmaster, and the school is beyond.

Ludgrove was, and still is, a family affair. The current Headmaster is a member of the family that founded the school and have run it ever since.

In Harry's day, one Headmaster was not enough! Two, Gerald Barber and Nichol Marston, were in charge in his day.

Although he did get a reputation as a bit of a handful, not enough to merit two headteachers!

It is a haven for an outdoors child. Woods abound, and sport is all. Rugby, football, cricket are the main sports, but there are opportunities for the boys in many others.

The school day is long, with lessons ending followed by a bit of free time, tea, and prep. As a full boarding school, the atmosphere is relaxed. Even back in the eighties, although more formal than today, Dotheboys Hall it was not.

Endless playing fields spread out from the main buildings, and sport is played every day. Most Wednesdays and Saturdays would see matches against other schools.

Diana was a regular attendee at these and would sit or stand quietly supporting the boys. Teachers and parents of the time remember a delightful, friendly and approachable lady who clearly loved these opportunities to spend time with her boys.

Just like any other parent, in fact, who had the financial independence to choose such a route for their children.

On other weekends, exeats would take place. On these days, school ended early on Friday and the boys would have the weekend with their parents.

But when at school, lessons continued on Saturday mornings.

Ludgrove would later have the challenging task of dealing with Harry's loss of his mother.

It had taken a while for him to settle, which would be the case for many young children moved out of their home environment into a school.

But he gradually came to terms with boarding life, getting himself involved in the odd jape and more regular scrape.

Teachers who came across him from other schools (Ludgrove staff were sworn to secrecy) report a polite boy with a cheeky look in his eye.

He had a tendency towards the immature, often associated with the youngest in a family. But not every youngest has the expectations of his lineage cast upon him.

With an early birthday in the school year, the starting point of which is September 1st, Harry was fractionally underage at Ludgrove. He would have always been one of the youngest in his year group.

He, therefore, repeated his final year before moving to Eton. Although not planned for such, it provided a year of familiarity following his mother's death.

Following Ludgrove, he followed his brother to Eton College. Once again, it took a while to settle. Eton was known in the late nineties as a privileged, but tough school.

The sons of aristocracy and the rich were expected to get on with life, to develop a hardiness which would stand them in good stead for their futures as leaders in their fields.

Harry again took a while to settle. He was not a natural learner in a school where academic expectations were high.

He had just lost, very publicly, his mother. It was a specially hard time.

Like all boys of his age, he again got himself into some scrapes, but these were largely kept out of the public domain.

One matter that was not was a claim that he had received unpermitted help for the A level in art. This proved not to be the case, but it cast a pall over a young man whom the press was beginning to categorize as the wild one of the royal family.

Whilst William, often against his mother's wishes, had been trained for the throne from a very early age and had so developed a calm manner (in public, certainly), Harry had been allowed more latitude when growing up.

His fiery hair added to the stereotype.

Rumours of a tendency to have a bit too much alcohol – even as a twelve-year-old at Ludgrove, of running naked in front of guests at a party for his father, and experiments with cannabis began to abound.

The extent to which they are true, exaggerated or completely fabricated we shall never know for sure. But do they matter?

Certainly not now, with the figure he has become, and even then, what teenager has not challenged authority?

A former security guard once observed that you never knew what to expect from Harry, but it was not said critically, more with a smile.

Harry did not particularly enjoy Eton. As we saw earlier, the change of schools came for him after a very difficult time of his life.

Repeating a school year is never easy for a pupil. There is never quite the same sense of belonging as with your previous peers.

And that was on top of the impossibly difficult personal time that he was going through, following the loss of his adored mother.

Some of his peers at Eton found him a little smug. He later said that he wanted to be a bad boy at Eton College.

But he left the school with two A levels. University was not attractive to him, and he decided to join the military instead.

Expectations would have been there that this would be a route he would follow even if he went to university first. But Harry had grown up with an interest in the military.

Zulu, which encounters a battle between a British Unit and Zulu warriors in Africa, was his favorite film. He used to watch it curled up with his father.

For a young man with a lot of energy to burn, with a love of the outdoors and a passion for sport, the army offered a perfect career opportunity.

Prior to that time, Harry would take a gap year. His love of horses and riding saw him spend time on a ranch in Queensland, Australia.

He also spent time in Lesotho, visiting (among other things) an orphanage for children suffering from aids.

It was a cause that had been dear to his mother's heart and soon would become important to his own life.

It was a tough childhood for Harry. One that had started brightly, but was plagued by his parents' failing relationship, then a troubled adolescence, something that he would take many years to face up to.

But by then, Harry would be a very different man.

Chapter Three - A Mother's Baby

'She was the best mum in the world. She smothered us with love, that's for sure. I miss having that mother to give you those hugs and that compassion that everybody needs.'

It took twenty years from her death for Harry to be able to say those words. In the intervening time, emotions were locked inside of him, following the death of his mother in 1997.

We will return to those awful events later, but for now, let us look at the relationship between Prince Harry and Princess Diana.

It was an extremely close one, even for a relationship between a mother and her youngest son.

'It was that love that even if she was on the other side of a room, as a son you could feel it,' he said.

The closeness between the two began before Harry was even born. Diana hid the fact that he was a boy from her husband, Prince Charles, fearing that he would want a girl.

Charles apparently expressed his disappointment to Diana's mother, Frances Kydd, at Harry's christening, saying 'We were so disappointed – we thought it would be a girl.'

And immediately after Harry's birth, according to Diana, he exclaimed, 'Oh God, it's a boy. He's even got red hair.'

Of course, the import of those words depends greatly on the tone with which they are said.

During the final six weeks of Diana's pregnancy with Harry, she and the Prince had experienced one of their closest times. During her pregnancy with William, Charles had found coping with her sickness and discomforts challenging.

But he had worked hard to be more understanding and knowledgeable when it came to her second pregnancy.

Sadly, the moment he was born, in Diana's eyes, the marriage fell apart. For Harry, those early days with his mother were intensely close.

'All I can hear is her laughter in my head and that sort of crazy laugh of where there was just pure happiness shown on her face. One of her mottoes to me was you know "You can be as naughty as you want, just don't get caught."'

As we saw earlier, Harry got himself into scrapes at school, to which Diana took a benevolent stand. In a letter written shortly after he joined Ludgrove, she wrote about her sons that they were,

'well and enjoying boarding school a lot, although Harry is constantly in trouble.'

Diana tried as much as possible to keep her time with her sons private. But pictures, especially ones taken at Thorpe Park (a theme park near London) and on skiing holidays demonstrate the deep love between them.

One of Harry and William laughing uncontrollably in the front of a boat on a water ride is particularly telling. No amount of setting up would reveal such a truth.

Harry was just twelve when Diana died. The circumstances around the death were tragic indeed.

But there were also deeper reasons for the impact on Harry to be as great as it was.

Diana was in a relationship with the playboy son of the Harrod's multi-millionaire owner Muhammed Al Fayed at the time.

Dodi Fayed, though, was not a man to whom either boy particularly warmed. They had spent some time on his yacht with their mother, but it had been uncomfortable for Harry and William and they had been glad to get back to their father in England.

It was the school holidays – William was by then at Eton, Harry in his final years at Ludgrove.

The paparazzi were at their worst, pestering the holiday makers, annoying the boys and constantly invading their privacy with photographs.

That had continued after Harry and William had returned to England, and even when Diana and Dodi returned to France.

As is well reported, Diana and her boyfriend had felt trapped in a Paris hotel. They had sneaked from the back into a waiting Mercedes and driven off at high speeds.

Although details are still unclear today, it seems as though they were followed by a paparazzi car, and entered a Paris tunnel where the driver lost control of the car.

It crashed. Dodi and the driver died at the scene. Diana was taken to hospital, but her internal injuries were too great, and she died, aged just thirty-six, on the final day of August 1997.

She had spoken to her sons earlier in the evening of her death. It had not been a particularly good call.

Both William and Harry had been doing other things, and each gave just a cursory few minutes on the phone to their mother, something both came to regret when they realized it was the last conversation they would hold with a mother they adored.

Although it earned them much criticism at the time, The Queen, Prince Charles and Prince Phillip kept the boys out of the public eye in the days immediately after Diana's death.

The media and much of the public criticized the Queen in particular for this. There was an enormous outpouring of emotion towards Diana.

The public felt they should be the arms of comfort to her sons. A bizarre reaction when seen in the context of time.

Why would two young boys want to have their private grief exposed to the world?

The Queen was portrayed as cold for her actions. What we can see how, in hindsight, was a willingness to take criticism – some vitriolic – in order to protect her grandchildren.

If the Queen and Prince Philip were regarded badly, then Charles was turned into the readiest target for the public's and media' anger.

It was almost as though he had been responsible for Diana's death. It led to the Prince falling to a terrible low in the eyes of the public. His approval rating crashed to just over 20 percent.

Yet, as we see now, he was doing the right thing. He was a comforting presence for his sons at the time they needed him most.

Harry said later that he was there for them, doing his best.

After a few days, both Harry and William were taken to London, to Kensington Palace, where the floral tributes became a sea of sadness.

The next time Harry was seen in public was at his mother's funeral. Rumors are that it was Tony Blair's idea for the young boys to walk behind their mother's coffin.

Whether it was or not will probably never be fully known; if it was Blair, it is a decision that he will have regretted in hindsight.

It was the most public of funerals. Hundreds of thousands lined the way, and Harry had to be persuaded by his grandfather to step out.

'If I do it, will you walk with me?' he said to his grandson. Only in the internment, on a small island on the lake at Diana's family home, did Harry have the opportunity to express his emotions in private.

Althorp House, which is in Northamptonshire, is where his mother now lies.

The impact of losing his mother took a severe toll on Harry. A much greater one than he realized.

He became the 'bad boy' during his time at Eton, and frequently appeared in tabloid exposes as a young man.

His reaction to the death of his mother was to bury it. Thinking about her made him sad, so he never properly grieved, not until many year later.

He buried his memories deep in his mind, in a attempt to cope.

There were, though, other constants in his life. His Grandparents, his brother, and his father.

It has been said that relationships between Harry and Prince Charles were at times strained.

What relationship between and father and son doesn't have its moments?

But actually, the reports are wrong. Harry and Charles have always been close, and that bond grew stronger as Harry entered adulthood.

It was Charles who broke the news to Harry and William that their mother had died.

'He was there for us,' said Harry many years later. 'He was one of two left.'

Charles himself was brought up to regard his duty to the nation, through his role as heir to the throne, as paramount.

It is true that he found some of the wilder excesses of the freedoms Diana allowed her sons to cause an eyebrow to raise, to say the least.

Nonetheless, he was a close dad to Harry and William. As close as could be when having sons who were away at boarding school from an early age. Also for many of their school years he and his wife were living apart, so holiday access was also limited.

He took Harry, the keen sportsman, to the World Cup when it was held in France. At the time, the formality with which the Prince of Wales is associated earned him criticism.

Harry was wearing a suit, rather than a baseball cap and t-shirt, as would have been the case had his mother taken him.

At least that was the impression. What the reporters who offered their negative views failed to say was that Charles and Harry were to meet the French President on that occasion, and formal attire was required.

Diana was constantly photographed hugging her sons, a giant smile on her face. Charles is always more formal in official photographs.

But that was how he was brought up to act. There is a photograph taken when Harry is 12 or 13. The boy has that look being forced to do something he really doesn't want to do.

William has a hand reassuringly on his shoulder, and the Prince, dressed in a kilt and leaning on a stick, has that frustrated look any parent knows when their child was being recalcitrant.

But in private, Charles is a warm and loving parent, now grandparent of course. Hugs, silly voices and funny faces from his father were a part of Harry's childhood.

That has grown into banter and teasing as he has grown up.

Charles was away from home more than he would, in all likelihood, retrospectively wish. His charity work was building up while his sons were growing, and he dedicated much time to this.

But, following his own upbringing, he did his best.

Tiggy Legge-Bourke, although distrusted by Diana, became a close nanny when Charles and Diana separated, and the relationship she achieved with both boys was remarkably close.

After Diana's death, he appointed a former Welsh Guards Officer, Mark Dyer, to ensure that a male role model would be around when he was not.

All remain great friends twenty years later.

Harry's relationship with his Grandmother, the Queen, has always been an interesting one. The two are close, but Harry still holds the monarch in awe.

He sometimes feels unable to match up to her achievements. When on an official duty, perhaps to a place the Queen had visited years before, he wonders how match up to the standards she set.

He sees her as much as his boss and his grandmother. When his brother William was at Eton, he would take tea with his grandmother at nearby Windsor Castle.

That was a far less frequent event for Harry, who was undergoing his 'terrible teens' at this time.

The Queen, though, is deeply close to her grandson. He reminds her of her husband, in more ways than one, as we shall see below.

His relationship with his grandfather, Prince Philip, has always been easier. The two are closer in personality than some of the more reserved members of the Royal Family.

Both Harry and Philip love a joke and like to be taken as seen. During the very worst days of tabloid excess, some stories were circulated that Harry was not Charles' son.

That James Hewitt, a love of his mother, was his father. The sole basis of that unpleasant suggestion is shared red hair.

That the dates of Harry's conception and their relationship did not match up and that both Diana and Hewitt completely denied the allegation did not dispel the scurrilous accusations.

However, a picture taken of Prince Philip from when he was around the same age as Harry, which appeared on the cover of a French magazine, confirms the truth.

Philip and Harry are the spitting images of each other; they have more in common than just their personalities.

Perhaps the strongest family ties Harry holds are with his brother. Right from birth, William adored his little brother.

Diana wrote about the fact that the toddler would smother his smaller sibling with hugs and kisses, and would not let his parents near.

Although William and Harry hold, in many ways, different personalities, that closeness remains. Harry struggled when William first went away to boarding school, not really knowing what to do with his time without a big brother with whom to play.

Siblings often come close together when there are home problems, and that was certainly the case with Harry and William.

They did not want to know about their parents' relationships; Harry, though, was more open to meeting Diana's boyfriends than his older brother, he was also more prepared to learn about his father's long time love, Camilla.

The siblings sought solace in each other at the time of their mother's death, big brother William being an enormous comfort to Harry.

That closeness has continued right to the present. William was prepared for his future role as King from a young age, while in some ways Harry was offered more freedom.

Perhaps that is reflected in their personalities. William was the bigger terror of the two as a toddler, but now his years of training is apparent.

He is a tad more formal, a little more reserved when meeting the public than his younger brother, who seems so much more natural.

But both men are a product of their mother. They have taken the monarchy forward together, with the father also playing his role, to a much more modern institution.

It is more in touch with the real world. It recognizes with greater clarity the good it can do supporting charities, raising the profile of good causes and highlighting wrongs.

It still plays its part in the more formal aspects of its role. It will be interesting to see if the balance further shifts once the Queen has stepped down.

Once again, further changes could be on the horizon after Charles' time as King.

Harry and William, often with Kate, frequently appear together. As children, the boys were often dressed the same, especially on formal occasions.

It must have been frustrating for two people seeking their own identities. Nowadays they do not dress the same but do share values and beliefs that are a credit to them, and their parents.

We will look later on some of the charitable activities they do, again often together. But let's end this chapter with a reflection on two brothers who are the best of friends.

Who support each other, each in their own way. And for William, the more senior of the two in terms of the royal family, he has a supporter who is 100 percent with him.

And who is also the most amazing uncle to his children.

Chapter Four – Military Life

Harry's time in the military marked some of hi

most controversial times. It was also the time

where he did much of his growing up.

It was a time where he finally realized that the

was something with which he needed to come

to terms.

And that was the death of his mother.

Prince Harry passed the necessary tests to ente

Sandhurst, the army's officer training center, ir

September 2004.

The tests are designed to enable the Regular

Commissions Board, or RCB, to determine

those who will be best suited to officer training

They consist of an assessment of mental, physical and emotional aptitude and potential.

Sandhurst remains a bastion for those from Public and Independent School backgrounds, with almost half of its intake coming from the nine percent or so that attend these institutions.

He entered the academy in May 2005 for the forty-four-week course, under the name of Officer Cadet Wales. Then, on 25th January 2006, Clarence House announced that he would join the Blues and Royals.

He was commissioned in April 2006 and the ceremony was watched by his father and stepmother, Camilla, Duchess of Cornwall.

The Queen and Prince Philip also attended.

The Blues and Royals was a sensible choice for the young prince, with his interest in horses, as they are a cavalry regiment, which comprises the Royal Horse Guards and 1st Dragoons. They are a part of the Household Cavalry.

The Colonel in Chief of the regiment is none other than the Queen, and Princess Anne is their ceremonial Colonel.

Bit of a family affair, then. But Harry was determined from the outset that this would be a distinct career move. While it is traditional for princes to join the armed forces, it is often for a short time. Harry's career would span ten years, and see him involved in direct action in war zones.

Harry's older brother, William, joined at the same time. He had completed his University studies at St Andrews in Scotland prior to joining.

The Blues and Royals is unique in that it is the only Regiment to be known officially by its nickname.

It plays a very large ceremonial role, involved in such events as the Changing of the Guard. Soldiers dressed in their characteristic tall helmets, red plumes descending, breast plate, riding boots and with ceremonial sword are a regular site in Windsor and Central London.

But as well as performing its ceremonial duties, the Blues and Royals is an operational unit. It took part in the Falklands War, provided support for the UN in the Balkans conflict, and has been active recently in Iraq and Afghanistan.

Following his induction into the regiment, he began training on his role as a troop leader. This included spending time at the Armour

Centre in Dorset, and working on signals, driving, maintenance, and gunnery.

After this, he returned to the regiment's base in Windsor, taking charge of eleven men and four reconnaissance vehicles.

Then, towards the end of 2007, he was posted to the British contingent in Helmand, Afghanistan. Helmand was, at that time, a volatile environment, with many British casualties suffering, particularly from IEDs (improvised explosive devices).

The posting was kept secret initially, amidst fears that such a high-profile target would not only endanger Harry but his fellow soldiers.

But the more irresponsible elements of the press allowed his presence to leak out.

Clarence House announced, with rather rigid formality and a sentence ending preposition:

'Prince Harry is very proud to serve his country on operations alongside his fellow soldiers and to do the job he has been trained for.'

Soon after his arrival in Afghanistan, he was promoted to Lieutenant with the Household Cavalry.

However, these leaks to the press and the distressing willingness of some to put commercial success over safety of its subjects meant that his tour was cut short.

Returning to the UK, he embarked on Army Air Corps pilot training and qualified as an Apache pilot in February 2012.

That gave him the opportunity to return to active duty.

While in Afghanistan for the second time, he participated in direct fighting with Taliban insurgents. Serving as an Apache helicopter co pilot gunner, he fired at targets.

'The squadron's been out here,' he said, 'Everyone's fired a certain amount. If there are people trying to do bad stuff to our guys then we'll take them out of the game.'

Being in Afghanistan was refreshing for Harry in a strange way. For once, he was just one of the guys. Other than attracting the odd look in the canteen, he was treated no differently to the other men.

There was no luxury room, he slept on a narrow single bed in a tent, just like other soldiers.

While in Afghanistan, his antipathy towards the press came to the fore. He was interviewed by the BBC's Royal Correspondent Nicholas Witchell.

He told how angered he had been by the press revealing he was in Afghanistan on his first call of duty there. Those details had caused him to be withdrawn from the country because the risk to British soldiers was too great.

On his return in 2012, any reporting was only agreed if the press guaranteed not to publish until his tour was over.

During the interview with Witchell, he is seen clearly looking around, watching what is going on. Then, soldiers begin running, and he leaps out of his seat to board his helicopter ready for more action.

He was in Afghanistan when the news broke that he would soon be an uncle. Once again, he states his wish that the media should leave the pregnant Kate alone.

He disabuses the many stories that he sent a letter from the front line offering congratulations. He points out that this is yet another media fabrication.

'They're wrong, as always,' he says a mixture of amused resignation and frustration on his face.

Later, in the interview with Witchell, he shows off the apache helicopter which he now calls his 'office'. It is cramped and complex. Among the skills he has mastered is peeing sitting down.

He talks about the buttons on his console being of different temperatures, to save having to look down at them.

His pride at his work is written on his face.

But serving in the military did more than invoke pride in the prince. It was the point that allowed him finally to confront the issue that had stood long and painful in his mind.

It was serving on the front line that enabled him to confront the emotional impact of the loss of his mother.

And from there, to become a driving force behind the mental and physical health of injured soldiers. But more of this later.

Harry recalled the horrendous images and experiences he encountered while in Afghanistan. He regularly flew the injured, civilian and military, to the hospital at Camp Bastion.

The sight of dead children killed by roadside bombs and injured, dying and dead soldiers scattered on the ground is the stuff of nightmares.

He had left Afghanistan looking forward to seeing his own family, but sharing the plane with desperately injured servicemen reinforced the reality of the conflict.

Most of the wounded had been caught by IEDs.

'Loss of life is as tragic and devastating as it gets, but see young lads – much younger than me – wrapped in plastic and missing limbs, with hundreds of tubes coming out of them, was something I never prepared myself for.'

Harry finished his army career with an administrative army role as a staff officer and completed a secondment to Australia, before returning to civilian life. It was, he said, a really tough decision to end his career.

By then, he was captain. More than this, he had become a man with a perspective and a purpose in his life.

Chapter Five - Controversy and Discovery

Remember, Harry wanted to be known as a 'bad boy' at Eton College. He was always a little on the wild side.

His bad boy image continued after school and through many of his army years, before his experiences on the front line led to a reappraisal of his life. A period of reflection that would lead to the man he is today.

One of the first major scandals with which he was associated came when he entered his twenties.

Attending a friend's party, along with his brother, he responded to the theme of

'Colonials and Natives' (itself, somewhat derogatory) by wearing a swastika armband.

Inevitably, although the party was private, pictures were taken and leaked to the press. The Sun newspaper, owned by Rupert Murdoch, published the story along with a photograph of the prince, attired in his costume, holding a drink.

William had chosen to wear an animal outfit.

Harry apologized for his 'error of judgment' after the event hit the headlines, causing a scandal. Clarence House also offered a statement of apology.

Jewish agencies accepted the error of judgment from a young man. Of course, on the one hand, it was a private occasion and, as tasteless as it may have been, everybody should be allowed time to be themselves.

Many young men have carried out far worse acts. But, the other side of the argument is that, as a member of the royal family, a prince is in the public eye.

That comes with all sorts of privileges of wealth, influence and opportunity, but carries responsibility as well.

There were consequences to the actions which went beyond what might have occurred had the arm band been worn by somebody else.

Ten hate crime incidents were reported to the Community Security Trust, which has a responsibility for monitoring anti-Semitism. Each mentioned the Prince specifically as a justification for their perpetrator's actions.

Harry's error of judgment was particularly embarrassing for the Palace because it happened in the run-up to the 60th anniversary commemorations of the liberation of Auschwitz.

The Queen was to attend that ceremony.

During his twenties, Harry was no stranger to controversy. He made a public apology after a video was released in which he referred to colleagues at Sandhurst in racist language.

A little later, his actions made headlines once again, although this time the public was on his side. He had been hounded by a member of the paparazzi, and his patience finally blew outside a nightclub in London.

A scuffle ensued and the photographer received a cut lip, which was largely viewed as his just desserts.

However, the red-faced angry prince was once again tabloid front page news.

In 2012 he was in the news again, photographed naked in a Las Vegas hotel where he was apparently playing strip billiards. Presumably, a kind of posh version of strip poker.

However, Harry was relatively unrepentant. He said it was a case of him being too much 'army' and too little 'prince', but, as he said, it was a private occasion and even a prince should be entitled to a little privacy.

And, to their credit, the public was by now much less entranced by tales of royal wrongdoing, many seeing the behavior as high jinks from a young man, rather than the start of the downfall of the monarchy.

Perspective was being restored, bad news for the more scurrilous elements of the tabloid press, at home and overseas.

It was soon after this point that Harry began to realize that he needed to address his trapped emotions regarding the death of his mother.

Later, in the period coming up to the twentieth anniversary of her death, he would recognize that he was in a bad place during his twenties, that there were emotions trapped deep inside of himself that were causing problems.

He began to understand that he had shut down his emotions in the period following her death, and he had not allowed them to start up again.

His brother, Prince William had tried to help, advising him to seek support, but little would assist him to address his problems. Things came to head when, as a twenty-eight-year-old man with a good army career he was conscious that he just wanted to lash out whenever anything went even slightly wrong.

At the same time, royal engagements were becoming an increasing source of anxiety to him. He felt that he lived a life constantly open to scrutiny, and had no privacy.

He had been conscious of coming close to a complete breakdown on many occasions. Harry was in his early thirties when he chose to speak about these terrible emotional problems openly.

He felt that to do so would help to bring into the open the mental health issues that both men and women suffered from.

Those that were hard to put into words, or about which people could be open. Finally, he realized that his brother was right, and he needed professional support.

He sought counseling, and took up boxing to find an outlet for his anger. It worked, and he found his world steadily improving.

Reflecting on the twenty years since his mother's death, he said:

'I can safely say that losing my mum at the age of 12 and therefore shutting down all of my emotions for the last twenty years has had a quite serious effect on not only my personal life but my work as well.'

He told of how he felt overwhelmed by the confusing conglomeration of grief, lies, and misconceptions that bombarded him from every direction.

His way of coping was to block out all thoughts of his mother because they were too painful to contemplate.

The boxing he took up provided an important outlet for the build-up of aggression he experienced over these years.

The anger he let out at the photographer outside a London nightclub would have been repeated more often had he not had someone wearing pads in the boxing ring to absorb his anger,

But when, following counseling, he began to feel able to stand up to these emotions, and talk about them, he realized that he was not alone.

That his stresses and anxieties were shared by many. He discovered that his brother, and others close to him, were correct when they said that bottling up emotions, and pretending to be immune from outside events, was not normal.

It was something that he needed to address.

Harry explained that his feelings that to think about his mother would be pointless – it would not bring her back – infiltrated all parts of his life.

He decided that emotions would not play a role in anything that he did.

'I was a typical 20, 25, 28-year-old running around going "Life is great" or "life is fine" and that was it,' he explained.

And then the grief began to intrude, and eventually, she realized that he needed help. Harry considers himself fortunate that it was only two years of what he describes as 'total chaos' before he found the courage to talk about it.

'I just couldn't put my finger on it,' he said. 'I just didn't know what was wrong with me.'

He developed a fight or flight mentality, one which made royal engagements particularly challenging. On these, 'flight' was out of the question, so he had to work through his pain.

But then he began to talk to friends about his feelings. He soon discovered that these friends had their own issues. Talking openly himself encouraged his friends to do the same.

There was understandably much speculation that Harry's mental health problems could relate to his experiences in Afghanistan. After all, we are learning all the time about the terrible impacts of post-traumatic stress disorder (PTSD).

But Harry is sure that this is not from what he was suffering.

'I can safely say it's not Afghanistan related. I'm not one of those guys that has had to see my best mate blown up next to me,' he explained.

'Luckily, thank God, I wasn't one of those people.'

No, for Harry, it was the experience of losing his mother in tragic circumstances when he was still a young boy that was the key.

That the entire event took place in a circus of public interest and scrutiny added to the problem.

However, Afghanistan had played its role in helping Harry to understand his feelings and to learn on the need to address them.

He worked with the personnel recovery unity and there listened to wounded and sick soldier discuss their own serious mental health problems.

It proved to be a turning point in his understanding of his own issues. He learned of the huge merit of talking about emotional and mental problems.

He learned that keeping things internalized only made them worse.

And he recognized that it was not just the individual directly involved who suffered, but also those around them, those who are closest to the victim.

'You become a problem,' he said. 'I, through my twenties, was a problem and I didn't know how to deal with it.'

Another thing that Harry discovered during his difficult twenties was about timing.

He explained how his brother was a constant support, encouraging him to seek help, assuring him it would be right to do so. But he knew that the timing had to be right.

He needed to feel that it was the appropriate point to discuss his issues with somebody, and find the right person to do so.

It is perhaps a sign of how much he had grown up post Afghanistan that he was prepared to hold what must have been incredibly difficult interviews so publicly.

He appeared not only in the press but on television advocating the importance of talking about mental health issues.

Harry believed that timing was right once more. There was intense public interest in the twentieth anniversary of Diana's death.

The recent birth of William's children had intensified attention on the princes. If they could talk now about the difficulties they had experienced, it could really make a difference to people's lives.

He stressed to the public that, if they had their own mental health problems, they should seek support. Hiding things away only made them worse.

But, he said, once they had taken the step to reveal their difficulties, people would be amazed by how much support was available.

He added that sufferers would be astonished by how embracing people were, and how quickly the difficult process of talking would begin to deliver results.

Harry was conscious of the moment. It would not be long before the public's interest in him and his brother was replaced by fascination for the next generation of royals.

He had to do his bit while the time was right. From leaving school to reaching the twentieth anniversary of his mother's death had been difficult for Harry.

The outward, confident and fun-loving prince hid a secret, one that he could not reveal. But in fighting for his country, he learned to fight for himself.

To bring his mental health problems to the fore, to seek resolution for them and them to help the public by sharing his experiences.

The future began to look rosier for Harry, especially in his personal life.

Chapter Six - Love is in the Air

At the time of writing this biography, the news was abundant in the media that Prince Harry is about to pop the big question to his girlfriend, the actress Meghan Markle.

The Canadian, who is three years older than Harry, has been the prince's partner since early in 2016, and rumors are abounding that an engagement is about to be announced.

Indeed, some papers have reported that 'royal sources' have indicated that the news has already been spread amongst Harry's immediate family and that a public announcement is imminent.

Whether that is simply story mongering amongst a press desperate to print something upbeat among the depressing stories regarding Brexit, or whether it is a story based on a reliable source which will be proved in the coming weeks is open to question.

However, it is definitely the case that the two, Harry and Meghan, seem extremely close. Indeed, the Jamaican idol and sprinter Usain Bolt says that he has never seen a happier Prince Harry than the smiling figure currently carrying out his duties.

Then, Harry has good reason to be happy. He is coming to terms with his personal demons regarding memories of his mother, he has just fronted another incredibly successful Invictus Games.

While his brother rightly spends as much time as he can be a father to his young family, Harry is becoming a serious face of the Royal family.

He is working closely with former US President Barack Obama, speaking at events and actions the former leader promotes and supports.

We are dealing with speculation, but sources reported to the British newspaper The Daily Mirror that Meghan was aiming to take a break from her acting career.

She recognized that if she is soon to be a princess, she will not have time for the body of work she currently undertakes.

She is best known for her role in the US legal series, Suits, where she plays the glamorous Rachel Zane. But she is also very involved with charity work, spending time supporting UNICEF in particularly.

It seems as though she is planning to spend more time on this as she waits to become an official member of the Royal Family.

Rumours even suggest that the question was popped during a trip to Botswana in August. Meghan accepted, but with the twentieth anniversary of Princess Diana's death at the end of that month, Prince Harry's sense of timing told him it was the wrong time to make an announcement.

If true, the couple seems to be set on a life in the Cotwolds. Prince Charles' Highgrove Estate is situated in this region, and it is known that Harry loves that particular part of the country.

Meghan is also reported to be wooed by the honey stone charm of the area.

Whilst it is believed that the couple has been seeing each other since at least June 2016, they made their first official public appearance together and the Invictus Games, where Meghan took a break from filming Suits.

The games were held in Toronto, which is where the filming takes place for the series. Toronto is also the home of the actress.

The media frenzy has been driven as far as raising speculation about the royal engagement ring. Apparently, it will feature a large diamond, with smaller examples of the stone clustered around.

The current interest must create mixed feelings in the prince. There must be a degree of pleasure that the media coverage is positive.

Also, that keeping him in the forefront of public attention allows him to spread his charitable messages, especially those around mental health, more widely.

At the same time, he would not be human if he did not sometimes hold the wish to be left alone. We do know that Harry holds the same frustrations with much of the media as his father.

And his mother. Indeed, being constantly filmed as a boy when with his mother must have been deeply intrusive.

Then the stories that emerged in his twenties will have further damaged his trust of the media. However, he seems these days to have developed a way of using the media to his advantage.

Long may that continue. Then again, were he to read a story breaking in one of the more unreliable red tops in the UK, he would be annoyed.

The story is reported here to give an idea of the kind of gossip and unsubstantiated claims that must be the cause of such infuriation to royals.

Apparently, Harry's stepmother has joined forces with his sister in law to break up the royal relationship. Completely overlooking the fact that Harry and Kate get on well, and Harry has a good relationship with his stepmother, the fabrication continues.

The joining forces of the two royal ladies apparently came about because they fell out over an alleged push from Kate to see William crowned king when the Queen leaves the throne.

Umm. That's certainly likely to carry weight! So, through an unexplained and completely unsubstantiated jump, their disagreement led them to attack Meghan, whom they dislike.

(Apparently, according to no-one with any knowledge of the matter.)

Should he read the story, and it is certain that even if he did, he would give it no credence an find it a cause for laughter, he might still take comfort from the ludicrous nature of other stories surrounding this one.

No newspaper can be taken seriously when it is prepared to print such scurrilous nonsense and over-hyped non-stories as these.

That there is a 'breakthrough' in the tragic tale of Madeleine McCann – how the girl's parents must feel when they see such nonsense seems to count for nothing.

That a TV show has had a 'boob fail' – that will send the world's economy into freefall!

And finally, a 'story' about a little girl blowing a kiss to a lion in a zoo. And that is just about it. A heart-rending quote from 'a user' is attached.

'The people in all these zoo videos are way more trusting of the glass barriers than I feel they should be.' Journalism at its best.

But hopefully, the above example illustrates the deeply annoying way that the gutter press seeks to make money from nothing, lazily and thoughtlessly printing much as it like.

But to return to Meghan Markle, she was born into an entertainment industry family. Her father is a lighting director.

Her mother is a psychotherapist and yoga instructor. She comes from a wealthy background and was educated privately. The is a college graduate, with a degree in theatre and international studies.

She got an insight into the diplomatic life in which she may soon be embroiled – as a part of her studies she spent time in the US embassy in Argentina.

She has been married before, to the actor Trevor Engelson. They divorced after nine years.

When the news of Meghan's relationship to Harry became public, she was subjected to even more personal harassment than the story outlined above.

The press launched racism and sexist attacks on her, to the extent that the palace was forced to issue a statement telling them to 'pause and reflect' before issuing such nonsense.

Of course, there are benefits to being a royal, but there are unprecedented disadvantages as well.

It is not surprising that Harry said that none of the younger royals particularly wanted to become the monarch, just that it was their duty to do so.

Meghan is not Harry's only romantic liaison. There were several short relationships during his twenties. Perhaps the first serious one was with Cressida Bonas, whom he dated for a couple of years.

She, too, is from an entertainments background, being an actress, dancer, and model. She was introduced to Harry by his cousin, Princess Eugenie, in May 2012.

The pair parted amicably in 2014.

And, dear reader, by the time you get this book, the truth of whether Prince Harry and Meghan Markle are to be, or have even become, married, will be known.

Chapter Seven – Charities

One among the many things that endeared Princess Diana to the nation was her commitment to charity work.

It did not matter whether the cause was big or small, she would gladly give her time and reputation to raise the concern in the public eye.

She was perhaps best known, in charity terms, for her work with Aids sufferers. At a time when so much misinformation existed about the condition, she changed the public's perception of the disease completely.

To achieve this, she did what any caring person would do. She visited an Aids center and held the hand of a sufferer. With that one act, the Princess turned the oil tanker of public opinion and demonstrated that Aids was not transmitted by touch.

She was also closely associated with the atrocit of landmines in previously war-torn regions of the world.

Prince Harry, along with William and Kate, ha taken the mantle held by his mother and commits an enormous amount of time to good works.

One of the causes close to their mother was Diana's support of African charities. She was, for example, patron of the Chipangali Wildlife Orphanage which supported African wildlife threat.

And it was following her visit to Angola in January 1997, led by the HALO trust, that she became the figurehead for the elimination of landmines.

Harry is heavily involved in charities associated with the continent. He has taken forward her opposition to landmines, calling for their elimination by 2025; he was also the patron of the HALO trust's twenty-fifth anniversary appeal.

Combining his commitment to Africa and his mother's support of Aids and HIV sufferers, he is the patron of the African children's charity, Sentebale.

This aims to support the mental health of physical well-being of child victims of the disease, direct and indirect, in Lesotho and Botswana.

It provides both cares to deal with immediate crises in the children's lives but also plans educational programmes to help them in the future.

And, it aims to ensure that these children are not discriminated against for their situation.

Prior to setting up Sentebale, he worked in Lesotho during his gap year.

As a part of her campaign to make people realize that Aids and HIV were diseases just like others, Diana had taken her sons to visit Aids sufferers.

It made a huge impact on Harry in particular, and this cause is close to his heart still today. In fact, he participated in a public HIV test with the singer Rhianna.

This was in Barbados and aimed to encourage others to take the test to limit the spread of the disease.

Diana was a patron of Centrepoint, the homeless charity.

Anybody visiting London in the 1990s cannot fail to remember and be touched by the cardboard village that existed beneath the concrete surrounds close to Waterloo Bridge.

Today, that area is home to teenage skateboarders, but back then the place was filled with the despairing cardboard shacks of the homeless.

As with Aids, Diana made sure that both her sons got to know about this condition. The gulf between living in a palace, and living in the freezing cold open air, prey to thugs and hooligans, hit both princes hard.

It is William who took up the mantle of Centrepoint, and he even spent a night living on the street. The cause remains close to both brothers.

The concert they organized, Concert for Diana, at Wembley Stadium to mark the tenth anniversary of her death, raised money for the charity.

One of the appointments Diana had arranged in 1997 was to Bustamante Children's Hospital, in Kingston Jamaica.

She never made it. But Harry did, fifteen years later. Even after his planned time was up, he refused to leave spending time with the young patients and staff.

It was his first solo royal tour, and was at the time of his deepest personal troubles, but nevertheless, his compassion was clear for all to see.

Harry's mother was also a patron of the charity Headway, which works with sufferers of head injuries. Her son opened their new headquarters, in Nottingham, in 2013.

But there are also causes which are close to Harry's heart which he has developed on his own.

WellChild seeks to provide care for the most seriously ill children in the United Kingdom. It also helps to transform homes so that these children can be with their parents.

He is their patron of the charity, which includes ambassadors such as Duncan Bannatyne, the businessman and former Dragons' Den member, Karen Brady and singer Alexander Burke.

MapAction seeks to provide mapping services for humanitarian aid for emergencies. One of the difficulties of dealing with emergencies is that they often occur in the most remote and inaccessible of regions.

MapAction tries to ensure that help arrives to those who need it as quickly as is possible.

There are numerous other charities with which Harry is involved as patron or supporter. He takes part in events such as polo matches which serve as fundraising events.

The Royal Foundation of The Duke and Duchess of Cambridge and Prince William was created initially to support the charity actions of the two princes.

Later, William's wife, the Duchess, joined. The organization exists to maximize the impact of the charity work, by creating a forum in which ideas and funds can be shared.

Of the many charities with which Harry is associated, we will finish with one born out of the personal experiences of the prince and his brother.

Heads Together seeks to open up issues of mental health. It promotes the power of conversation and openness in overcoming the problems of mental health illness.

Subjects such as bereavement, the problems of childhood and trauma in the workplace are clearly concepts close to Harry's own experiences, and he, his brother and the Duchess are passionate about promoting this openness.

They are significant forces behind World Mental Health Day and have used their influence and contacts to get many celebrities onside, including the singer Lady Gaga.

Heads Together became the Charity of the Year for the 2017 London Marathon, and the princes' own openness in discussing, on television, their own mental health issues following the death of Diana helped to demystify and remove the stigma associated with the commonplace, but secretive, condition.

Although the charity is young, it has led to the creation of extra counseling services, the use of creativity to address mental illness and has linked with other charities to strengthen its impact.

It is hard to think of a better benefit a prince can offer that help to address a problem that is common, global but treatable – if people are prepared to talk about it.

It is too early to consider legacies for a Prince who is just thirty-three years of age.

But he has, through all of his charitable work, made a significant mark on people's lives.

That is how royalty can offer good these days. That is a modern monarchy serving a very important function.

Harry is central to that.

Conclusion – What does the Future Hold?

Who can be sure what the future holds for Prince Harry? When the Queen, for whatever reason, steps down, then his brother will assume even higher importance in the line of inheritance.

As the next heir, William will be driven by protocol and expectation, just as Prince Charles has been.

But the incredibly close bond between these brothers seems certain to endure. Harry has stated that he has no wish to become monarch.

It seems as though he will be happy with his lot as a man able to do so much good through his charity work.

Somebody who can perform public duties with an ease and a smile that warms the nation to him.

Hopefully, those years will continue with a partner by his side. Possibly, even probably, that will be Meghan Markle.

But we cannot be sure. What we know is that Harry has turned from the lovable rogue of his younger years to an inspiration for a generation.

We started with a look at his personal venture, the Invictus Games. Let us end with this remarkable event.

Michelle, as you will recall, suffered terrible post-traumatic stress disorder as a result of her role as a medic in Afghanistan.

It ruined her relationship, her self-worth, her life. She turned from a professional woman to a lady whose demons were so strong that, in her forties, she would wet herself at night.

She was at the point of ending it all. Prince Harry's creation of the Invictus Games changed her. It gave her a purpose once again, membership of a team she thought had gone forever.

'When I look in the mirror, I see the glint again, she says.

What a wonderful thing for a man to inspire.